WILDFLOWERS OF OREGON

Photography by Steve Terrill
With Selected Prose & Poetry

Oregon Littlebooks

Westcliffe Publishers, Inc.
Englewood, Colorado

First frontispiece: Silver dollars along Wahkeena Creek,
in the Columbia River Gorge, Multnomah County

Second frontispiece: Yellow tree lupine,
with Humbug Mountain in the distance, Curry County

Third frontispiece: Bracken fern and mountain arnica,
Salmon-Huckleberry Wilderness, Clackamas County

Opposite: Penstemon on a cliff overlooking Wizard Island,
Crater Lake National Park

International Standard Book Number: 1-56579-121-5
Library of Congress Catalog Number: 94-62087
Copyright Steve Terrill, 1995. All rights reserved.
Published by Westcliffe Publishers, Inc.
2650 South Zuni Street, Englewood, Colorado 80110
Publisher, John Fielder; Editor, Suzanne Venino; Designer, Michelle R. Reeh
Printed in Hong Kong by Palace Press

PREFACE

The first light of the new day bathed the wildflower meadow in a warm golden glow, reflecting the morning dew and making the scene appear as if it were a field of precious gems. To me it is always a magical experience to find such an array of wildflowers. The glistening dew drops, clinging to every leaf and stem, intensify the surrounding colors like thousands of tiny diamonds.

When I chance upon a setting such as this, I could — and many times have — spend most of the day photographing it. Each individual water droplet acts as a primitive lens, mirroring the meadow and the wildflowers behind it. And in each drop I discover anew the wonder of nature.

I step back and see a dragonfly drying its wings and readying for its daily aerial acrobatics. A few feet further is a brightly colored yellow-and-red western tanager, swooping down in hopes of starting the new day with some insects for breakfast. A breeze picks up and the wildflowers and grasses dance back and forth, sending some of the morning dew back to the rich soil of mother earth.

As the breeze subsides and the flowers return to their stately pose, the only movement I now see is out of the corner of my eye. This must be my lucky day, for not only is the light now creating what is known as a halo effect around the flowers, but it is also highlighting a white-tailed deer browsing on the edge of the meadow.

Later in the day as the sun warms the earth, the fragrance of the wildflowers is released as a heady perfume. This, combined with the mesmerizing sound of bees searching for pollen in seemingly every flower in the field, creates a sensation that one has to experience first hand.

I do not think my imagination could conjure up the beauty of a field of lupine and Indian paintbrush surrounding an alpine lake, with a

Evening primrose below the Steens Mountain, Harney County

snowcapped mountain looming in the background, its image reflected in the clear, cold water. Or standing in the heat of the high deserts of central and eastern Oregon, parched regions where yellow bee flowers cling to life as they send their roots deeper into the cracked soil to seek out precious moisture.

A haunting yet unforgettable experience that I have encountered in the late spring and early summer months on the slopes of Mount Hood is when fog enshrouds the mountain, draping the forests and fields of rhododendrons and bear grass in a ghostly mist. I imagine that I am in a prehistoric world, and the swirling fog reveals what appears to be an animal, but in reality is only a tree. The tree then disappears as rapidly as it appeared, fading back into the cloak of wet fog.

I love these mystical moments in the mountains, yet I am equally drawn to the beauty of the Oregon coast, with its endless varieties of wildflowers and its sweeping vistas. The dunes, cliffs, and hillsides are abundant with flowers, mainly during the late spring and early summer along the southern coast. Here you can see fields of pink and white foxglove, yellow tree lupine — with plumes five foot tall! — and cliffs thick with white cow parsnip, some with clusters the size of dinner plates. Vibrant yellow gorse lines the roadways.

The abundance of wildflowers is one of the reasons why I love to photograph in Oregon. Whether I'm shooting in the mountains, along the coast, or in my own back yard, there is always something new to discover, a special moment to experience. It is these moments that are preserved in the pages of this book. I hope you enjoy experiencing them as much as I have.

—Steve Terrill
Portland, Oregon

Woolly sunflowers beside Triple Falls, Columbia River Gorge National Scenic Area

"The earth laughs in flowers."
— Ralph Waldo Emerson, Hamatreya

Field of lupine, buttercups, and Indian paintbrush,
Mount Hood Wilderness

"One of the attractive things about the flowers
is their beautiful reserve."
— Henry David Thoreau, Journal

Rabbit brush beside Crump Lake,
Hart Mountain National Antelope Refuge, Lake County

"To create a little flower is the labour of the ages."
— William Blake, Proverbs of Hell

Weathered tree trunk and Indian paintbrush,
Mount Hood National Forest, Clackamas County

"I should like to enjoy this summer
flower by flower"

— André Gide, Journals

Wild peas blooming along the southern Oregon coast,
near Brookings, Curry County

"Flowers . . . are like lipstick on a woman — it just
makes you look better to have a little color."
— Lady Bird Johnson,
Time magazine, September 5, 1989

Monkeyflowers among granite boulder,
Eagle Cap Wilderness, Wallowa County

Overleaf: Yellow pond lilies in Douglas Lake, Eagle Cap Wilderness, Wallowa County

"Nothing is so like a soul as a bee. It goes from
flower to flower as a soul from star to star,
and it gathers honey as a soul gathers light."

— Victor Hugo, Ninety-Three

Peach orchard and wild mustard,
Marion County

"Beauty is truth, truth beauty—
that is all
Ye know on earth,
and all ye need to know."

— John Keats, Ode to a Grecian Urn

Dame's rockets,
above the Columbia River Gorge, Multnomah County

"Flowers are words
Which even a baby may understand."
— Arthur C. Coxe, The Singing of Birds

Wild daisies, Coos County

"Work — for some good, be it ever so slowly;
Cherish some flower, be it ever so lowly…"
— Frances Sargent Osgood, Laborare est Orare

Yellow bee plants beneath the Painted Hills,
John Day Fossil Beds National Monument, Wheeler County

"Nothing in the world is single,
All things by law divine
In one spirit meet and mingle."
— Percy Bysshe Shelley, Love's Philosophy

Cow parsnip along the coast,
near Newport, Lincoln County

"Shed not tear — O shed not tear!
The flower will bloom another year.
Weep no more — O weep no more!
Young buds sleep in the root's white core."

— John Keats, Faery Songs

Teasels and blackberry vines covered in frost,
Grant County

"How does the meadow-flower its bloom unfold?
Because the lovely little flower is free
Down to its root, and, in that freedom bold."

— William Wordsworth,
A Poet! He Hath Put His Heart to School

Field of foxglove, lupine, and daisies
Clackamas, County

Overleaf: Balsamroot, with Mount Hood in the distance,
Hood River County

"Throw hither all your quaint enamell'd eyes
That on the green turf suck the honied showers,
And purple all the ground with vernal flowers."
— John Milton, Lycidas

Penstemon on Summit Rock,
Winema National Forest, Klamath County

"Beauty is its own excuse for being."
— Ralph Waldo Emerson, The Rhodora

Dogwood and cottonwood trees,
Columbia River Gorge, Multnomah County

"And 'tis my faith, that every flower
enjoys the air it breathes."

— William Wordsworth, Lines Written in Early Spring

Pink monkeyflowers beneath Mount Jefferson,
Mount Jefferson Wilderness, Marion County

"To see a World in a Grain of Sand
And a Heaven in a wild Flower,
Hold Infinity in the palm of your hand
And Eternity in an hour."

— William Blake, Auguries of Innocence

Gorse flowers along the coast, near Bandon,
Coos County

"Flowers have expression of countenance as much as men or animals. Some seem to smile; some have a sad expression; some are pensive and diffident; other again are plain, honest and upright..."
— Henry Ward Beecher, Star Papers: A Discourse of Flowers

Bear grass, Mount Hood National Forest,
Clackamas County

"A charm that has bound me with the witching power,
For mine is the old belief,
That midst your sweets and midst your bloom,
There's a soul in every leaf!"
— Maturin Murray Ballou, Flowers

Water lilies,
Polk County

"The loveliest flowers the closest cling to earth...
The happiest of Spring's happy, fragrant birth."
— John Keble, Spring Showers

Balsamroot on the Rowena Plateau,
Columbia River Gorge National Scenic Area

Overleaf: Honesty flowers and a lone scotch pine, Multnomah County

"Spring lightens the green stalk, from thence the leaves
More aerie, last the bright consummate flower."
— John Milton, Paradise Lost

Butterweed and monkeyflowers along Crater Creek,
Deschutes National Forest, Deschutes County

"Beauty is a primeval phenomenon, which itself never makes its appearance, but the reflection of which is visible in a thousand different utterances of the creative mind, and is as various as nature herself."

— Goethe, From Eckermann's Conversations

Field of lupine,
Multnomah County

"You must not know too much, or be too precise or
scientific about birds and trees and flowers . . .
a certain free margin . . . helps your enjoyment
of these things."

— Walt Whitman, Specimen Days

Foxglove on Cascade Head,
Tillamook County

"The Amen! of Nature is always a flower."

— Oliver Wendell Holmes,
The Autocrat of the Breakfast-Table

Lupine and monkeyflowers along Elk Cove Creek,
Mount Hood Wilderness

Rhododendron, Table Rock Wilderness, Clackamas County